IN EROS AND CHAOS

RANI HIRANI

To you, with love.

Contents

Contents

Acknowledgements

I would like to express my gratitude to my online readers and friends across the globe for heartening my work and showing all the love that keeps encouraging me. You guys make me believe in myself, without you I could never start my writing journey in the first place. Special thanks to Rishi for reading my first draft and supporting me from the very beginning.

I'm so thankful to Revo (Biru Panda) for making this beautiful cover and being an affable friend that everyone needs.

Above all, thanks to my family for having their faith in me.

I love you all so much.

1. Poet's darling

I didn't hear anything against you,
I chose not to listen.
Now I am a homeless wolf that all the forests have forbidden.
You used my vehemence to get over your hurting,
I use your indifference to write my poetry.
In these verses, I will bleed forever from the parts of my skin I
could never cut.
I will keep scribbling your name until the day I no longer feel
any emotion,
Until the day my poetry loses its metaphor and personification.

Though I still can't hear anything against you,
I will never listen.

"You will always be my home, out of all the places
forbidden."

Love story

I felt love ever so ardently

That winter night for the first time

When I saw through your soul

and you carved its fragments as mine.

Glimmering in the dark days,

warming our heartaches,

we were like sailors of two ships that didn't care about reaching the

shore,

at least not anymore.

and it was enough,

Following a path highlighted with your name
It led me into a trench,
more profound than my imagination.
We both chose it without any notion.

Sinking, diving, and sometimes choking
We created a home filled with raspberries of lush spring and lusty
winter's red wine.
Scented with sweet vanilla and the sourness of lime.
But with you, two years isn't enough in any lifetime.

You and I, we aren't the sun and the moon
We're the dripping blood and the scribbled ink.
A blend of sweetness and bitterness.
A hardened passion and fragile rawness.
Yet everything that can fill the yen of our parched tongues,
Our wrecked hearts, our dark souls.

Blissful sin

In the graveyard you burry your parts,

when your house is a mansion full of atrocities,

What shall I call you,

a fallen angel or a helpless devil?

in both ways, *you are a blissful sin.*

"Strolling in Eden's garden with a lover's arm around the shoulder is a wish of many,

But would you play with me on the swings of a lonesome playground during twilight and watch it turn into a sacred place weeping in the torture?"

Fingernails

Sipping coffee on my balcony as I flip through the collection of
letters that I've written till now,
my mind thinks about so many things, all related to you. Like the
way you get lost in the depth of new places and how you're always
alone but never lonely.

Entranced by your beauty and the structure of your fingers that I
yearn to hold ever so gently.
Your existence resembles overwhelming poetry that can make the
dead feel alive in the graveyard.

Darling, you scare my melancholy and rip its heart out with your

fingernails,

you turn the blues of my soulless existence into a field of

sunflowers filled with liveliness.

Not that I believe in magic but with you, I do desire a fairy tale

where we can sit underneath the moonlight as I play your favorite

song.

Sweet illusion

It is a dream.

It is a delusion imprinted under my skull

just like your name is imprinted on the walls of my heart,

making a border that doesn't allow anyone but you.

It is a temple carved from a rock cliff,

created with the divinity of tender love and a yearning so true
blue.

You say our worlds are different but mine starts and ends with
you.

Lullaby

I press my lips tenderly against his forehead

and like a euphonic lullaby it lulls him to sleep.

He closes his eyes and his long lashes resemble the crescent moon.

Here lies my moon, my prettiest constellation

and my own little universe of affection, admiration, and

adherence.

- he is a tranquility that comes after torment.

Touch

I melt in the fiery soothe of your touch
as your fingertips dance slowly on my belly.
Subdued under your nectar,
I gaze into your impassioned eyes.
They tell me the kind of story that I needed in my life.

Not to tell the world about it,

But to keep it to myself,

and to know about a soul so fervent

that taught me a love so deep-rooted.

Locked between the cages of my ribs

now there's a volcano that screams your name

and I live my way through life on the rhythm of it.

Your lips greet my crooks ceaselessly and

my bones feel like a safe secret embraced by your body.

-When a bare touch feels like home.

Evermore

Who was I?

I was-

a shattered heart consumed by triggers,

but your soul found love in that.

An old painting with faded figures,

but you saw your favorite colors in that.

A lost letter, bleeding its ink,

but you found your unspoken words in that.

A star-crossed shore where all the boats sink,

but your strings made a bridge for that.

So now I make my soul your devotee and display your portraits on

my walls.

I write uncountable letters to you,

I promise to wait for you until you reach the shore,

until you hold my hand forever and evermore.

- Telling your stories to the ocean.

Persephone

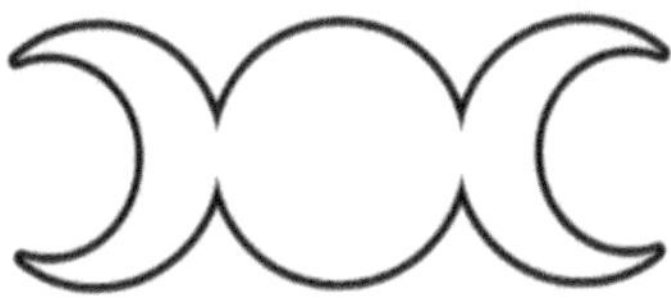

I write to you my finest letters with vintage pens,
Your name is written on every page of my diary, surrounded by
hearts from a red sketch pen.
The shade that matches the lipstick stain on the collar of your
white shirt.
You used to worship me like an Aphrodite,
I became a Persephone
and accepted your world as mine.
Now the darkness stays rent-free beneath my eyes,

night passes into daylight as tears tell our stories to my pillow,

making their way through my cheeks.

What makes me still waiting for you?

Hope.

"A fragile hope that's half drunk on lovesickness slithering its way to you."

Hope

I love you in the distance

As much as I love you in my arms,

In the silence that surrounds us,

vicious as the chaos that destroys our hearts.

You are my hope, my light.

My secret prayer at night.

You are a little kid trying to hold back his tears,

a person of nobility with no fears.

When grief encircles your soul,

When your heart is shattered and sour,

Let me mend its fragments with the threads of hope.

-We are in this together.

Difference

According to him,

out of all the human emotions,

he is madness.

A psychotic mess,

a chaotic soul,

a walking dagger that will gash everyone who comes in his way.

A hungry beast starving for destruction,

A bottle of wine filled with poison.

But to me, he is just a human heart wishing to be loved.

A worn-out body begging to be held,

An unsteady mind yearning for sanity.

A lost wolf looking for his mate,

An old language, forgotten by its fate.

- You are normal and you deserve to be loved.

Rosy autumn

In this crispy autumn that is bringing us uncertain thunderstorms,

I will stay as patient as the sea,

especially when you need me to be

And I will read you my favorite poetry

while stroking your hair

And whispering in your ear that

"You don't need to live for people, but you must live for who you
wanna be."

For the sunshine that awaits to kiss your agony
and the glory of your heart that enlightens my soul,

I will be with you in every uncertainty.

Closure

Here I'm in front of a small window, on the evenings of rainy
June, writing about something for the first time that doesn't have
the forelsket of having you.
Instead, it's filled with the ache, remorse, and everything that came
along with the process of losing you.

It has the touch of our final goodbye, the one that we promised to
never speak of in this lifetime.
The crossed hearts are now scattered,
their hurting will never forgive us.
Until the day it totally forgets us.
But forgetting isn't easy, we know it better.
So here comes a question,
Will all the things show me your reflections in them or will it be
me searching for you wherever I go?
Whatever it will be, it will haunt my soul.
Like the time it did this afternoon when a lady played a verse of
our favorite song.
Taking me back to those lovesome nights of December.
Later on, it reminded me how someone else already remembers
you through them,
Soon they'll be the reason why you're happy again.

Things will change.

The color glaucous will lose its glitter
You'll like your coffee a little too bitter.
Will I search for another muse,
Another home, another soul?

I don't see it happening because,

you will be missed

in between the pages and the ink,

whenever I write, my words will scream your name,

for you are a poet's darling and will always remain.

2. Chaos

Loneliness has found its way to me in the most crowded rooms,
For it has loved me more than anyone.
And these voices in my head screaming,
How did it all go wrong?
What is the place where I belong?
The heavy-handed suppression of my emotions
dies by the heaviness of my cruelty.
My cruelty, took birth by insanity.
Not that I complain,
I tried embracing the chaos that made me insane.

Honey, now I'm digging my grave
Will you bring my favorite flowers?
Or will you even ghost the ghost of me?
The new people that you've found,
I hope they make you laugh,
I hope it makes you happy.
I hope your eyes glimmer and your cheeks turn pink,
a tear of sweet memories rolls down your cheek.
As you visit my grave,
Bringing my favorite flowers,
Calling my name.

Salvage

For a fleeting moment can I lose the weight of this vulnerability?

Fighting with your demons, I lost my sanity.

A marionette of yours who kissed your vanity.

Sipped your love in holy grail but it turned out to be poisonous,

You always stroll out of the door, leaving me all ruinous.

Whom should I go to and ask for the lost fragments of your love?

So that I can fix it and have you back.

So that I can fix myself and have myself back.

But where can I find something that never was there?

The glimmer of your eyes- oh so rare.

But the games of your heart could never be fair.

But for a fleeting moment, I wish to overcome this damage.

My life is a jailer, my soul yearning for its salvage.

The moon that witnessed our last clandestine meeting,

I ask her why the opposite of love is hating and not hurting

She smiles and says, it will hurt as long as you will keep choosing

it.

So here I'm bearing it,

choosing it,

all of it.

Another chance

I look into your eyes and I see your infuriating self that has the
ability to destroy anything that dares to come his way.
Love, my love.
You have always been so vigorous, right?
Slow dancing in the kitchen has turned into sleepless nights where
I cover my mouth with my palm and weep my silent cries.
Giving it another day
Giving you another chance.

But I know it'll never change
Not until I untie all the strings that are still attached to you.
Our pillow talk is long gone, buried in the graveyard right next to
the coffin where you enclosed your love and my soul still dances
with the ghost of it in agony.
Yeah you were always vigorous
but you never intended to harm me,
at least not in the beginning.
But the 'beginning' now seems so far.
Time flies and today my heart reminded me of a lesson that I
learned the hard way when I was a little girl.
I take deep breaths as if I'm her,
She exhaled "abuse can feel like love."

Midnight ghosts

Pancakes, honey, and strawberries
a morning of sunshine, warmth, and no worries.
You wore a little dress and bought
some white lilies.
Sat in the garden and read your favorite book.
Strolling through the city, eating your favorite food.
People watching and daydreaming about love as you write poetry.

But as the day ends you come back to the reality,
Burying yourself in your bed solely
with your midnight ghosts.
They await your shattered soul
to give it a new scar,
to peel off the layers of courage
that you have gathered so far,
To gag your mouth and take away the peace,
You plead, weep and shiver.
And again you're a haunted museum,
longing to be understood.

Cruelity

Saw you running down from stairs,
I secretly hoped you wouldn't fall.

Wishing for a hand to hold
but all you get are fazed stares

by people like me, people like him,
who have known you all this time,
All this time when nothing was right,
You were there in front of my sight.

Watched you ruining yourself,
I secretly hoped you wouldn't die.
Thinking you could rely on words,
But in the name of love, they all lie.

Heard you cry your loudest screams,
I secretly wished to wipe your tears,
You were there getting trapped by your fears.

The vulnerability that you wanted to embrace,
They called it a burden, what a disgrace.

But one day you will rise above this toxicity,

accepting your flaws,

owning your identity.

Rage

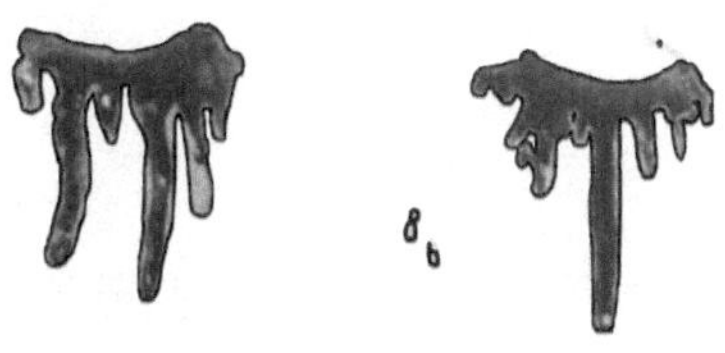

I bite my tongue until it bleeds,

it forestalls the words that I want to scream.

I hold my fist so tight,

my nails end up digging into my own skin,

this halts my hands from strangling so many.

Sweat bubbles on my forehead

as if someone has set my soul on fire.

My bloodstream gets sedated by my rage for it is more violent

than my personification

I become a vicious beast drunk in frustration,

Stronger than the alcohol that you tiple daily,

For you, it is a source of glee,

for me, you are my sweet agony.

- my muse is my agony.

Labyrinth

The numbness throbbing inside my head consumes the air before I
try to breathe in.

Exhausted, I keep running in the labyrinth that wasn't meant to be
mine but I never faint, instead I feel a bomb ticking inside my
chest so I beg it to end everything.

I imagine my flesh and bones tearing apart and my soul being
guided toward nothingness.

They lay my body under a beautiful cemetery and notice how
silent I am until they realize I've always been.

In my head among all the chaos, I secretly prayed for this

moment.

So, here ends the game of heartache,

the torture of life,

and the process of slow death.

But oh my agony, it never stops.

She finds her home in the heart of my beloved as they wail in my

loss.

- this kind of pain never ends

Her

What shall I write about her?

for she herself is the poetry

of love, heartbreak, and compassion.

Alliteration lingers around and she soliloquizes in her sacred
solitude.

The burning flames of her heart often sound like hyperbole to
others.

Simile walks hand in hand with her moon like enchanted soul,

unafraid of the darkness and brave enough to be with the wolves.

Irony, unholy-irony

poured in a glass of wine she sips with her lover.

A hurricane, sometimes a shadow.

What a disgrace it is to heal a heart and then break it,

to ask for love when you can't even take it.

An unfinished novel

In giving you what you seek, I forgot my needs,

Pleading you to stay, I am on my knees.

But you leave me like an unfinished novel,

forgetting it was written for you.

Perhaps if we had similar love language,

the greatest love of all time wouldn't remain unsaid,

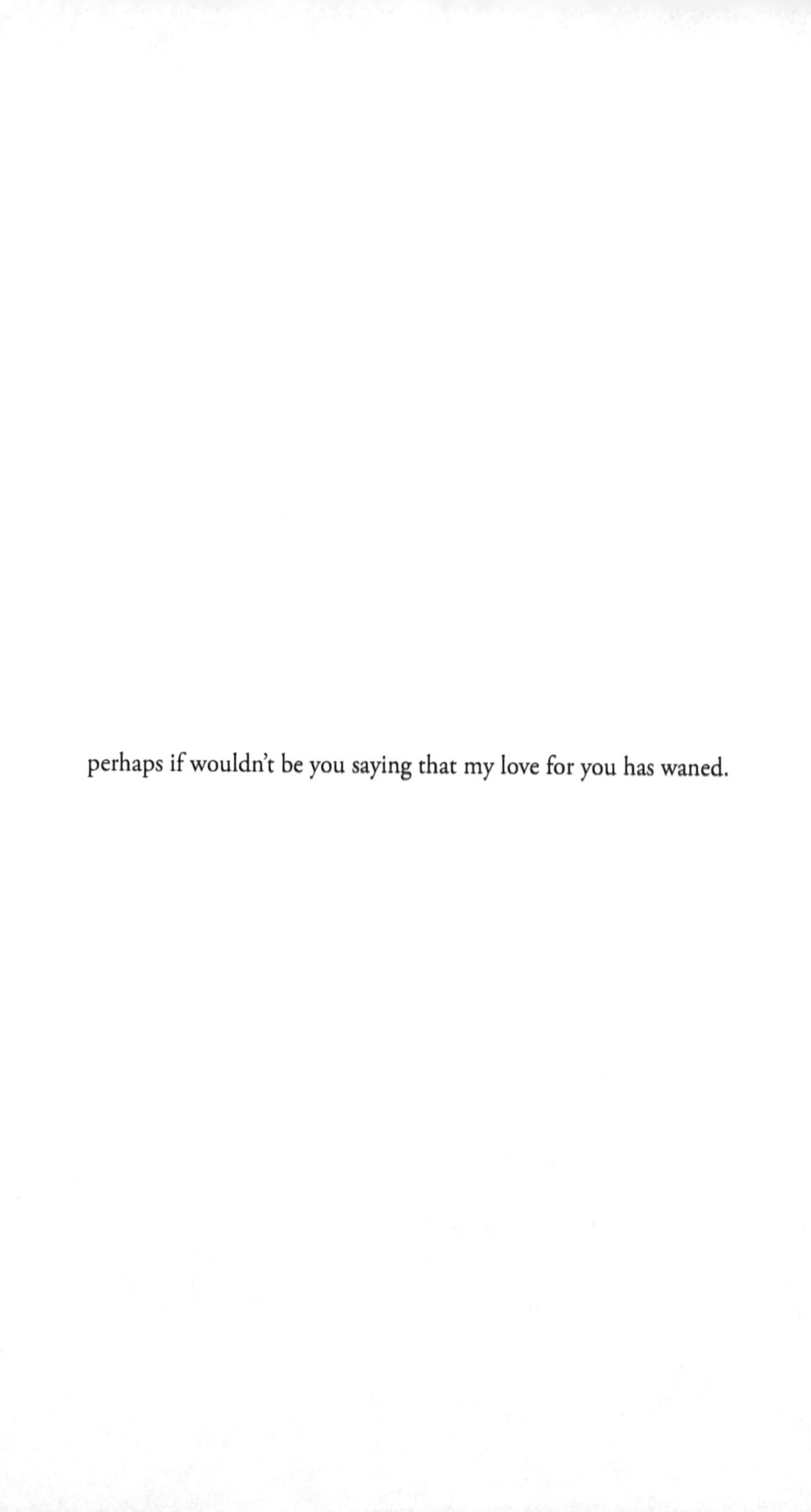

perhaps if wouldn't be you saying that my love for you has waned.

Unsent letter

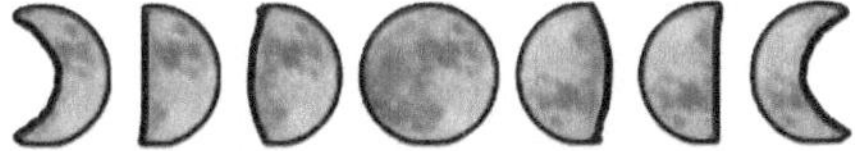

I lay all crumbled on the floor of her bedroom
where she wrote me for the first time.
Her smile was brighter than the stars
in the midst of that December night.
All the love and doodles of heart that I carry
are just a mere fraction of how she felt,
When butterflies danced in her belly
on the melodies of love in the air.
She kissed him on the doorstep.
Placed the flowers in the vase.
She told me how madly he loved her.
He was her favorite start.

But as the moon from her window
changed her shape.

Nights got darker,

Not even a single ray of hope to escape.

One day he walked out of her life

without even saying goodbye.

She tore me from her diary and

crunched me as if I was her own heart.

No mercy, so brutal.

It was the ending of her favorite start.

Now the roses have dried and the vase is broken.

I'm carrying the weight of words that will forever be unspoken.

She is walking over thorns and pieces of glass.

All the pain and words that I carry

is just a fraction of what she feels deep in her heart.

But what do I know about how she resents,

I'm just a love letter that never got sent.

Wanderer

Weeping in anguish, there was a wanderer so homeless

Searching for the footprints of affection

strolling a journey so homeless.

But he remains a slave of his paranoia and insecurities

until love caresses his cheeks,

All his fears surrender in front of it.

For now, he is no one's slave but a devotee,

growing and learning wholeheartedly,

Incomplete

Today I want to ask you something,
Today I want to know what you think about me,
And when it comes to me,
My thoughts define me more than anything.
Tell me, does my heart define me too?
A heart that has never been loved, is it able to love others?
Is it even able to handle the love when it knocks on its doorstep?
Will it accept that affection with open arms or will it hide under

the blanket,

Layers after layers until it is all suffocated and loses consciousness.

A mind that has only fed with abuse,

Does it know how is it like to be in peace?

From the beginning, it has given in to ruination.

And thus, it thinks peace can only be achieved with annihilation.

When a soul has never known its true singularity, it is lost.

In a crowd or in an empty room, it is always lost.

Searching for the impossible and hiding away from everyone.

Such fragments of mind, heart, and soul,

They remain incomplete,

Like this poem,

Like me and you.

Agony

Sometimes I'm drowning in the lake of nothingness, other times
I'm a crumbled-up paper torn from your favorite poetry book
because it held so much agony that the hardcover couldn't carry it.
But if someday, somehow you come across it,
will you touch it with your bare warm hands and tenderly fold it
in your pocket?
Will you read every paragraph with utmost devotion dwelling on
your tongue like you used to?

As you read it, will your brittle cold heart be warm again?
Will you feel the sensation of love over your melancholic strain?
Will you close your eyes and hold my hand,
when you realize what you left behind is still the same?

Destroyer

We often write about the people we love, making them the muse of our art.
For they are a source of light that manages to reach the darkest shallows of our hearts.
But what about the people we hurt?
About the homeland that got burnt in the arson committed by our own hands,
about the forbidden house that once was our home, about the graveyard that we used to worship that is now a place where our raw emotions are concealed?

Here is to the knocked-down sculpture that I used to worship, the one that I dismantled with my own fragile hands as if they were hammers aimed at a particular spot *(heart)* and crushed it into bits,
"I am no longer the person I used to be, all my roses have shed their petals,
I am left with thorns and I pierce all the hearts that try to console me. Just like you did mine, just like I ended up doing yours.
I'm a story that is unfinished, unloved, and probably prohibited by a lot of places.
By you, by all the places, because mine are the words that aim to destroy."
- Your destroyer.

3. Letters

Fifty days have passed and I'm still waiting for your letter
Wishing to unfold its envelope and smell the fading fragrance of
dry flowers that you might have attached,
I wish to read it so that I can feel better.
There is a hell of emotions burning inside my chest but it seeks
comfort in all the wrong places.
Perhaps, there are no right places.
Lately, I've reckoned, my loneliness isn't about being lost in the
crowd.

It's about people that I love pushing me away, fabricating the
walls around themselves, and forbidding me but not the world.
My friend, do you remember us cycling to the park?
Maybe give me a visit when I come back to that small town,
Maybe a hug to fix every wound,
Maybe a smile to ease my heart,
Maybe an effort to have a new start.
Till then I'll keep waiting for your letter,
Waiting for something to make me feel better,
Even if it takes forever.
I'll keep waiting for your letter.
I'll keep waiting for your letter...

Lover - 1

Love can be illusional but she makes me believe that it is real. The hurting, the ugly crying, the longing to spend the rest of our lives together, the waiting to hear from her at the end of the day, to look at the sky and think of her and **whisper her name like a soft orison**, it is all real.

When I'm holding her hand designed with fetching henna, *which by the way has my name written on it*. I'm giving her more than my trust and promises. I give her my faith for she is a goddess that deserves so much love.

To express affection in little things and an effort to understand the complexities is all it takes to make her feel loved. Though, such a pity it is to love someone and be unable to help them. The amount of helplessness that it imposes, is cruel enough to make your lungs stop breathing. It is when you realize *drowning Jack was less painful than Rose's agony of losing her lover in front of her eyes.*

Lover-2

We talk about the lost love, the one that breaks our hearts, the new love, passionate beginnings that bring butterflies in our bellies and blush on our cheeks as we hear the sound of their voice.

But what about the love that stays?

He met me exactly when I needed him but the best thing is that he stayed.

So here is to the one that chooses to stay and accepts the real you.

The one that adapts to your daily habits and makes them a part of their lives, the one that starts using your slang because you talk to them all the time, the one that gets jealous and is secretly possessive every time you talk about someone else with a smile. Maybe the one that's "meant to be" as the old ones say but the one that adds meaning to every step you take with them.

He met how waves meet the shore, washing away my sorrows and discomfort,

calmly touching the sand and whispering tales of divinity in my ear,

he soothed my very soul.

With my agony, he takes away my fears too, as we stay awake till 4 in the morning telling each other anecdotes of our lives and adding pages to our poetic love.

Exhaution

Dear workaholic friend,

On an unusual night like this, when you are just a tired person wishing to be loved because who doesn't need a touch of tender love kissing their temples, and a soft rub on their back saying it will be okay?

Your life is so bustling that you forget what is living. You work until your muscles are sore and stay awake till your eyes shut on their own, surrendering, 'This is enough'.
A foremost loner who has accepted the darkness, for it is a part of your soul. You try so hard to seek happiness but end up being acquainted with temporary sources of pleasure that enhance the void in your existence.
When you are stuck in traffic and your mind ponders,

whether it is a never-ending loop of misery and false hope or an abyss of delusional thoughts where you are running recklessly.

Whichever it is, take a deep breath and start your new day by giving affection to yourself wholeheartedly.

Enter Caption

November

Dear November,

I waited for you the whole year so that I could wear my favorite cardigan

but destiny took me to that part of the country where there is no winter.

You make me feel like a pale beast when I ask you for my defunct glister.

Homesickness eats me alive

as they feed on my peace of mind.

I see myself giving up all hopes steadily

The feeling of being unloved saddens me so badly.

Like a dry leaf, half dead in its misery,

I roam around in the city where the wind takes me.

The city of sunsets and beautiful history.

It welcomes me with a sweet stranger whose eyes have searched a
lot for me in the crowded rooms.

Those eyes greet me with a soft peck on my cheek

Those eyes speak all the hidden messages that I seek.

December

Dear December,

I'm not going to beg you to be kind after these eleven months because no amount of kindness can undo the wickedness that this year brought into my life.
So if you want to be something, be a crystal clear mirror and show everyone their real reflection.
The reality that they are hiding behind the sweet fondant of lies,

burn it with the fire of karma and let the ashes fly in the air.

When a dry leaf falls from the tree, it has no idea about where it is going.

So, to people who have no idea about where life is taking them, be a cup of hot chocolate with a small note that says, you'll be alright. Be a calm golden ray of sun as it sets and says goodbye because a lot of us never got the closure and buried a half-written storyline along with some parts of us attached to it.

*"Be a gentle fall of snow and answer the prayers of hearts that still have a little faith embedded in them.
Be true, be humble and be a lovely new year's kiss that leads to a doorway of new beginnings."*